She

– Stride –

Other Stride books by the author:

What the Black Mirror Saw
Orchard End
Abyssophone
The Laborators
Dressed as for a Tarot Pack

Sheen

Peter Redgrove

— Victoria & Don
— all best
— Penny

SHEEN
First edition 2003
© the estate of Peter Redgrove 2003
All rights reserved

ISBN 1 900152 87 8

Cover design by Neil Annat
Cover painting by Rupert Loydell

Acknowledgements
Haiku Quarterly, Kanto, The Manhattan Review,
Stride, Swansea Review, Poetry London,
Poetry Review, Poetry Wales

Published by
Stride Publications
11 Sylvan Road, Exeter
Devon EX4 6EW
England

www.stridebooks.co.uk

Contents

Sheen *9*
On the Cusp of Two Winds *11*
Various Caverns *13*
Incidents *15*
A Bearded Palace *17*
Prester *18*
Bells as Bioblasters *20*
Revenants *22*
Clouds and Rain *24*
The Spin of Trees *26*
Horizontal and Vertical *28*
The Artist *30*
Millennial Entreaty *31*
Seeing Things at the Lizard IV *33*
Coronation Stones *34*
Valet Toucheur *36*
Gentlemen *38*
Eve Naming *40*
Rank *41*
Spidermill *42*
The Grey Boat *44*
Tom as Supernatural Presence *46*
Jumbo Haiku *48*
Hatching *50*
Seance for Fu-Manchu *52*
Ecophilia *54*

Painted in Apocrines   *55*
Superwhite Extra-Large Perispirit   *57*
Invisible Until They Arrive   *58*
Working the Chain   *60*
Amethyst Rock   *61*
Woman Passing Through Book and Brick   *63*
The Bed   *65*
Spiritualism Garden   *66*
Took Her for the Gardener   *68*
Vine and Rain   *69*
The Hotel and its Juices   *72*
The Arrival   *74*
Astradame   *77*
Door Among the Dunes   *79*
Resin   *81*
Bearded Gold   *82*
Fey Body   *84*
Fall Graduate   *85*
Head Door   *87*
The Teaching   *89*
From His Time Machine   *91*
Poems Found in Commonplace Book   *92*
Cabala Mount   *94*
Caverns and Towers   *96*
Blue Cricket   *98*
The Font   *100*
Solid Prayers   *101*
In the Year of the Comet   *103*

The Boys Inside the Hills   *105*
Library Lab   *107*
Unpredictable Acoustic   *109*
Henrhyd Waterfall   *110*
On the Links   *113*
Dante by the Seaside   *115*
The Index   *118*
Comestible Orchestra   *120*
Scene Shifting   *122*
I Was Myself Again   *124*
The Handclasp   *125*
Lizard Moonscape   *127*
Observatory   *128*
Books and Vistas   *130*
Prince Plum's Furniture   *133*
Sweetness of Light   *135*
Three Bells   *137*
Portals   *139*
Passing Clouds   *141*
The Thrones   *144*
From the Good People   *146*
Gynandromorphism in Butterflies and Caftans   *147*
The Sublime Art of Reading With Books or Without   *150*
Zinc Bin   *153*
Floral Dentist   *155*
On the Dining-Room Shelf at Rock   *159*
Afterglow Laboratories   *161*

Peter Redgrove 1932-2003

Sheen

I.

A singular star
                fell from heaven – he
                              bound it hand and foot,
To nourish the biblical serpent
                that walks upright
                              like a sheen or glory,
The sheen the look of the sound
                of its scales on the ground
                              and the look of its hiss:
This pyrosome, the female firesnake
                coming to teach him
                              female orgasm
By her hiss, the Lamia
                in Griffon Glade at last.

II.

How gorgeous, the Arcadians,
                the liars pushed
                              into the Well of Truth
Containing the Water of Truth,
                              barely potable
in their velvet and lace collars,
                reclothed in water
                              simply add water and push

And the truth comes out,
                and it is dry water, shining,
                                their dresses did not
Get wet, but once emerging
                they could only tell the truth,
                                the speeding ghost that is all-water
Stilled, and speaking as one water.

On the Cusp of Two Winds

I.

Clouds full of salve;
                the orgasm, the hushed roar;
                              the parrot shows
His gallant eye to the tomboy Mothers
                whose coiffure has a rising soul,
                              a special sheen
Like an oversoul.
                A caulked sky,
                              dreamless dry lips;
A square-headed dog
                with batwing ears yawns
                              as a sentry yawns.
Electricity changing in the air
                slips something like a silk mask
                              off my face so I am
No longer a villain
                in stockingmask;
                              her orchestralle
Of sexuality awaits us both;
                she passes the time
                              by shaving her legs calmly
While the thunderstorm continues.

II.

The cloud-wrack copies
        the old estuary track, the wrist's
                moderate clock persists;
Old clothes chaperone him,
        humbly, sadly.
                The star
A conjurer's tap, pinned
        to black velvet nothing,
                turned full on,
Pouring from nothing.
        But she walks
                like her name walking,
She rests like an hour
        that is female only.
                Splashes of rain
Like moth-scales shed.
        A hill, a ladder, a horse –
                all my husbands.
The wind
        loves across the river
                in big espousal sighs.

Various Caverns

'…if thou sleepest upon a dunghill, it becomes
the church for the pouring out of prayers…'

He was in a great furrow,
                he was covered with mud,
                              embodied in it,
And that was his first wet dream.
                The darkness
                              weighed like the rock roofs
Until by crawling it was made
                of that velvet which
                              could be seen through the skin.
They levered their whole selves
                into the little slimy sump-hole
                              which narrowed dangerously,
The sphinx-sphincter
                before it enlarged
                              and became the Virgil Caverns.
The figures of counsel
                moved in the wall,
                              the visionary womb-arch rich around them.
Surely his companion in the adventure
                was one of those
                              who had come through the wall;
The vaults glossy with red mud,
                this was the Trysting Cavern
                              lined with fountains

Sparking with the light of
                his hard-on in her wide-on;
                              was their whole self;
The figures of counsel
                fluttered the wall
                              the visionary womb
Anarched around them;
                they shared the comfort;
                              usufruct, exterior cunt,
The moulding reflex in the mud,
                the hypnotism of its
                              millennial smell.

Incidents

The palace circus-hall
                and the palace laboratory
                              and the arena hosed down
For comic decorating, all
                the colours of the rainbow
                              must be manifested
In the curtains of whitewash,
                in the overalls that scream with paint;
                              this last
Is where the Prince comes with his
                clown-troupe in an opus
                              which is called 'erasing
The Royal Family' and is completely harmless;
                in the Silent Room there is only
                              a waxwing feeding
From a berry-laden mountain ash;
                and in the scullery the action-paintings
                              put to right, pressed
And ironed: the washing machine
                like a disordered church organ
                              spinning itself dry of that fluid,
Music; the sonorous acceleration
                like a small aircraft,
                              kittens of dust
Playing with each other in the spacebehind;
                after the sex-game

                        you can see everything
The corridor carved like a copse with
            silhouettes of children
                        cut into the golden heart-wood;
Royalty squeezed me
            and the currents flowed. She said
                        it was like embracing
A big old tree.

A Bearded Palace

A bearded palace
                persecuted the Princess
                              but her suit breathed power –
After the torrential rains
                the clear water of the harbour…
                              washed down from the hills
A cloud of mud expanded
                beneath its surface… originating
                              sand-dunes, innumerable lit
Cogs in one wheeling dune
                turning into the wind
                              and travelling
Up the beach;
                respiration
                              is from God:
'As that General
                which Knighted
                              his whole army,
God shall create us all
                Doctors in a minute',
                              in Donne, (Easter Monday 1622)
In dune.

Prester

I.

The eye which cleanses
                the ocean's deepest part
                              is blinking slowly,
Wafting the seas;
                when it weeps,
                              enormous tears
Overwhelm the islands;
                storms linger
                              in the water
Many days, serial clouds
                fall into the eye of ocean
                              creating thunder.
The atmosphere is the invisible
                supersea, the weatherfronts
                              are the lids.

II.

Came to that Island
                famous for irises
                              the voyagers.
There the tragic actor
                dedicated a summerhouse to the memory
                              of his brother,
The grounds of the theatre

      tremulous with storm engines
          and wind-machines
Bass as the storms themselves.
    As they performed
         the memorial play
The great iris of a thundercloud
      stopped the light down – nevertheless
         the scenes were
Sharper from the electricity
      of the cloud so charged
         it was called Prester;
The actors
     rode their wind-machines
        and thundersheets
Booming back at the opening gates
     of the palaces of cloud.

Bells as Bioblasters

To convoy with the setting sun
               through the dark valley,
                             to adjust the labours
Of the autumn sun;
               to raise power with the bells, to change
                             the look of the town
With the changes of the bells
               clearing the rainclouds away,
                             hollowing them away
By Kteis, by Phallos,
               by bell, by clapper,
                             to work for a bell-foundry
And be called 'sainterer'
               marrying clarity and power;
                             invisible bell-shapes
Jostle everywhere
               aerial medusa-shapes
                             travelling in the bell-notes
Rising and falling,
               the gothic bells pressing their amorous
                             shapes everywhere
'Marrying the sinister with the numinous;
               the sonorous with the numinous,
                             the sound of the reek of bronze
Shuddering from the towers,
               the great grove of bell-sound

                        shedding its audible leaves
The red sonata of autumn, the cool scorcher,
        the notes fall as the leaves fall
                all surfaces are metal for bells
Emitting their octaves, their spectra
        that drift into corners and corridors;
                this old wall vibrates with the bells,
Until the whole town is its single echo
        out of its one bell and clapper
                that fades into a charged silence
And after-echoes:
        a complex bell with rooms still singing,
                a resonance machine, this
Leafy grand hotel, this Kteis.

Revenants

I.

Children, the fruit of the night,
                the infant gods spirit-fed
                              and attended to in the dark;
A picture of ships moored
                during the day,
                          at night
It is a basket of flowers
                attended to
in the dark
                by giant bees with phantom wings;
                        a pebble
An impeccable ghost-house;
                a forest seen from the inside
                          as by ghost, and a woman
Asleep with her ear to the ground:
                'whatever the spirit that calls
                          a kindred spirit
will answer...'
                shudder the thought; some of it
                          is the radiant form of rubbish;
A mark still on my side
                where B died,
                          over the gall-bladder:
Eve's stigma.

I saw my mother
                    who has been dead
                                        ten years,
Strolling
                    on the other side of the street,
                                        the shady side,
Arm in arm with a good-looking man
                    not my father,
                                        and she was full of joy
Looking up at this man;
                    then she crossed the road
                                        to me and I
Was that man.

Clouds and Rain

'In love is the shiver of joy, and within the shiver is the flow,
and within the flow is the flow...' Evola

The parents' bed almost solid
        with dream aethyrs;
                the child thinks
The bedroom is haunted;
        actually it is the bed,
                a great Christ of Aethyr,
A Shiva machine
        for her small shaker
                of the universe, yet
I was her shiverer
        saw all her legs
                and the long antennae
Of her jewellery,
        their shafts of searchlight
                glittering all over,
The drops of water
        on her clothes flashing
                and in her Prideaux proudwater,
The same drops flashing
        in the dark light,
                the dark rain inside her.
It's shivery
        how the universe can
                like a great book

Be read in the bed,
>	turning the sheets,
>>		the dark clouds above full

Of dark rain
>	that turns to light
>>		in the flesh.

The water gathering like windows,
>	for her movements
>>		kept coming

And like a conjurer
>	I was to keep them wheeling
>>		with my rods and

Spinning plates
>	as the rain gathered and fell
>>		until I could spin them no

More, and I sped
>	through a tunnel
>>		of dark rain

Where I found I was changed, my skin
>	opening like an eyelid
>>		on the fountains beneath

Like fountains, we turn round and round
>	inside our mutual fountain,
>>		rain changing to cloud

And falling as rain again
>	in her shining
>>		chamber without corners.

The Spin of Trees

(From: Broken Ground)

The may trees,
        stilled
                whirlwinds of dew.
Look! They stop spinning;
        as you look away,
                the white trees
Spin again
        throwing out sane air
                brewed by the flowering boughs,
Into the rivers of air
        so clean and fine that polish
                round the mountain's bluffs;
Goddess-breath, balanced and silky;
        a vapour of stone from the cliffs
                smelling of stone
Is wrung out also; trumps blow
        off the ragged edges;
                walk in the wind
Between the fractals
        of the mega-cliffs,
                squint into a fine crack,
Survey the micro-cities
        quiet in the stone,
                bend to them making

A sound of the wind
                with the Goddess-air
                              haloing around your head.

Horizontal and Vertical
Stepped Verses at Twilight I.

In the mistral
                      – magistralis ventis –
                                        the mastering wind
He looked down at the birdshit
                      and saw writing;
                                        He saw the images dropping
From the vast reservoir
                      of the bird's tail
                                        stretched on the magister wind,
Collected from all the air:
                      gnat fodder, seaspray
                                        herring plucked like a flower,
White on black splash
                      like an open tome
                                        black splash on white, shit
From the fundament of bird-process
                      a greater spirit than what is visible
                                        using bird-alphabet,
Scaffolding of the air
                      secret grains of winds
                                        the furnace of the hollow bones
Forced draught
                      skeleton like a case
                                        of flutes hot from blowing
Out among the tombstones
                      splashed with their lichens

                              where a man with a bonfire
Was throwing old slate tablets
                on to the flames where they cracked
                                with hard detonations
He found himself
                reading the cracks
                                a flock of geese creaked
Overhead, the flight pattern
                of birdshit in formation,
                                and there was the birdsong
Tangled with the creaking boughs
                the bird sits on the branch
                                and sings to its creaking
Bird and bough duet
                as if it were a
                                flesh and bird violinist
With his wooden voicebox
                or the tree in the wind
                                sings to accompany the birdsong
And the bird sings according to breeze
                and not tree
                                alphabets of all genders
There are twenty-six genders
                that need to codify
                                the images of divination
Produced by the bird's angel from under its robes
                which is its flock
                                of rowing air, spattering song.

The Artist

The surfaces of water gliding past
                wide iron girders of the pier
                              rusted by the seawater
Have painted a perfect landscape
                with bluebells and a sunny sky
                              and turfy meadows, a coppice of trees,
The glimpse of a stately home
                reclining on its bosomy columns
                              among peeling autumn foliage,
All done in rust upon iron,
                the artist, Seawater; never still.

Millennial Entreaty

Smelling of the whole
        Middle-East, sherbert
                and nuclear devices,
A moon
        glances over the dreamers
                creating poetry
After their fashion in each.
        The earth shall reel
                to and fro like a drunkard
And shall be removed
        like a cottage,
                the hearth is broken,
You have broken it;
        heal the breaches thereof
                for it shaketh;
This operation is indeed
        a labyrinth
                for here present themselves
A thousand ways
        at the same instant.
                But your eyes
Shall see your teachers,
        your ears
                shall hear a word behind
Saying:
        this is the way,

                              walk in it, know
when you are to turn
                to the right hand
                              and when you should turn
To the left hand;
                (we are made to drink
                              the wine of astonishment
That we may do our work,
                our strange work,
                              and bring to pass our act,
Our strange act)
                see, I have engraved this
                              on the palms of your hands,
On the backs of your eyes.

Seeing Things at The Lizard IV
The Dark Rainbow

Two pulses – it was dusk
                and the lighthouse tower
                              commenced its wheeling light;
In a meadow at its foot
                a watersprinkler rose and dipped
                              catching the high beam
Of the tower, with this fan
                rainbowed as if painted, caught
                              the three-second
Swinging beam with its penumbra,
                fell back with a sigh
                              into the meadow grasses,
The lighthouse beats the air
                with this fan
                              into light, into darkness,
A fan and a fin made visible,
                and invisible when it swam back
                              into the dark
When you could see it
                only with its hiss in meadow grasses.

Coronation Stones

I.

When the true king
                was placed upon it,
                              this stone would cry out
with a large voice VIVAT!
                the shout unlocked
                              the fountain of the great deep
and the M4 flooded.

II.

Recalling to me the tale
                of the shepherd, Magnet,
                              who discovered lodestone
While tending his flock
                among the stacks of quiet
                            of the slate quarry
On Mount Ida –
                pieces of the stone
                              clung to the nails in his shoes,
Unsteadying him.

III.

So there was this knowledgeable pointing stone
                that opened the reign silently

                                  so that there was no shout
And the rivers remained
                sleeping in their beds
                          or stepping down
Their oozy staircases
                not letting the vocal
                          fatherspirit declare itself.

IV.

Lodestone, lodestone
                should be used, lodestone
                          with its burden of magnetism:
The second atmosphere
                of the mountains
                          that settled there untroubled
Until men came, noiseless
                burglar-alarm
                          to regal Mount Olympus.

Valet Toucheur

Shiva's quicksilver shiver
                electric city passing over
                              a man made luminous by thunder
'And studious of a self
                possessing him'
                              the echoes of his self
In every corner
                valet toucheur
                              the dark green fish
That at dawn vibrate
                the shady forest streams
                              and the Weatherfish
Or stone loach
                as the thunderstorm approaches
                              it is carnivorous
It thrashes eyes and teeth
                wildly on the surface;
                              the warty watery newts
With tails tapering to nought,
                the male in valet's
                              breeding dress,
Touch is unfallen,
                from the top of the stairs
                              comes the slow salaaming tick
Of a very old clock
                in mahogany case –

                                        time told
In the forest shade, my tree
                    wound by touch, wound.

Gentlemen

The town Gents
                flooded as usual,
                              by the chalice-fountain
Stained with birds;
                I went down into this pit
                              it was awash with libations,
Half-lit through knotted glass
                set in the pavement overhead
                              like a leaky battery
With stained plates and pungent packing
                just large enough for a dozen pissers
                              to piss nether electricity together;
Piss powerhouse
                water playing over stone;
                              so I climbed the stairs
From the one electricity to the other,
                sunlight winged with doves, wings
                              and all the hearts beating together
In the keels of their breastbones
                like winged ships,
                              rainwater off wings
And wings astonished at Gents
                rising out of the ground;
                              I climbed from one fragrance
Into another,
                the hiss of the feathers,

                                        the piss of the men
Men ascending and praising the sunlight,
                    the water-carriers, the men descending
                                        into the charged twilight, then up
To fill their eyes with water off stone,
                    water sunlit with dove-wings,
                                   visible electricity,
Water that gives us sight,
                    passes through, hisses,
                                        rests in the head-bone fountain
where the whole scene swims.

Eve Naming

Tree of light,
        thistle-tower,
                searchlights made of silver hair
They stare back
        with silk that is seed,
                combed beard of silk-seed
Sitting on all its thrones at once;
        green sepals grip the jewel
                which has turned
Into a rosette of semen;
        we blow some seed of it
                into a sunshaft
It skims in argosies:
        actual presences
                called out
From susceptible species –
        named or pointed out,
                they step forward
Spruced up by their name;
        she savoured the word thistle,
                and as she pronounced it
I saw it in a moment of silk.

Rank

Spiders of high rank,
Prince-spiders
Hurrying by with their velvet caps.

The bulls and cows of great rank
Passing by under their pavilions of mistbreath.

The grasshoppers, gracehopers,
Busy messengers.

The dogs, stalwart sergeants
With a livery of chest-and-muzzle
And saliva, medals of wet-nose saliva.

The cats or doctors
Teaching their gymnosophic stretches.

And each bird wearing
The crown of all birds.

Spidermill

Spun utterly clean
            the waterwheel
                        and the web;
The spider draws dew between its
            pincers, drinks;
                        the wheel a shining
Staircase of wood
            always descending
                        like creaking ghost-stairs,
It is a round cascade
            turning all night all day; spider's
                        wheel still as clockwork; who
Consumes yesterday's catch
            of tattered flags;
                        to start the day,
For thrift, devours the guillotine itself;
            once the miller's boy
                        slipped on the parapet
Was eaten by the woodwork:
            who can say 'beast'
                        of either construction?
The black spider rests
            in its white wide
                        security robes
Studded with ermine of moths,
            the lean spirits; while the small

                              spider spins
The wide court of its presence,
                the throne in its hindquarters
                                which it takes everywhere,
Baiting the trap which fills
                with goggling marionettes
                                on spiral strings
And salt staircases;
                very savoury wet crisp spirals,
                                both wheels full of stars
After their kind.

The Grey Boat

The naturalist's punt painted
                grey with a matt finish
                              to minimise his presence,
Seagulls folding themselves
                out of the sky
                              like clean napkins
Ironing themselves
                alight on the rooftrees
                              as for a miles-long banquet;
The rippling lights of water
                across the ceiling, the ancient
                              horsehair plasterwork;
The old well vaulted in
                at the end of a long stone passage;
                              prayer in the privet,
Stops for a moment
                aware of a listener,
                              starts again, the wind-hum
In the privet; who is the ghost
                where is she in the house?
                              he thought he'd go
Into the woods,
                and love his soul there
                              in the continuous Mass
Of transformation of the leaves, 'each stamped
                with an effigy of the tree'

            he would be the ghost of the tree,
The lime tree which drinks the rain up
      and hums with its bees –
            the hum, noticing something
Stops for a moment
      then turns on again;
            a shower of leaf-gold babies
Inset in the raindrops, struck out
      by the sun, gold Cabalah;
            a shower of it
Just over the grey boat
      and the lake.

Tom as Supernatural Presence
(For Tom) OB 9.9.99

A Guinness erect on the bar
                like a straight-backed pint
                              of black cat, full
Of black lights;
                the young black cat, he
                              is a dream-presence
Like a Guiness; it was as though
                the sealed books of his heart
                              burst open; he shot out
His bolts of warmth
                into my lap, the locked volumes
                              burst their clasp;
It binds me to him,
                he does it
                              more than once,
To ensure our friendship;
                then he glides down
                              and scuds away
Leaving my feelings aglow:
                a bonfire of animal heat
                              right up to my midriff.
I have seen him retexture his coat
                to make it fascinating;
                              it glows subvisibly;
Or he causes each hair

                    to declare itself separately,
                                    each like a black ray
From an invisible star; as though
                    it were the nerve-endings
                                    he combed with his tongue,
The plantations of blackness
                    rippling as with a night-breeze in
                                    the moment before the first
Star becomes visible;
                    and then a swift glance
                                    from the gold eyes
Like a ship floating painted black, lined
                    with its great cargo
                                    of pleated gold-leaf;
Or in the shadows
                    at the stair-foot
                                    this pair of jewels
Floating a few inches above
                    the carpet, as though darkness
                                    were crouching to inspect
For night-mice
                    at the house-root.

Jumbo Haiku

I.

Self-seeding and self-manuring,
                a garden that tends itself,
                              a lawn that rolls itself
With its own round lodestone,
                millstone cut out of the lighthouse ruins,
                              the gardens in
A state of arousal,
                working in their invisible mode;
                              smell them coming
Invisibly, then the rain arrives.

II.

After a long long journey,
                reaping my grey beard with my fingers,
                              combing out the journey
Teased out in feedback,
                the smell knowledge
                              recorded in the beard
Played back by spreading it out,
                restoring my tired fingers.

III.

A mirror and a barre
                in the fresh-painted studio,
                              the turps has blossomed
And gone away, the light staying
                              with the fresh paint,
Shadow-box, all shadows
                              painted away
The resonance
                of the freshly-painted air,
                              freshly-painted air
To dance on.

Hatching

(By the Old Powerhouse)

The tapping chalk of
                the new powerhouse eggs
                              muffled as if at a great distance
The underscratching within,
                the egg-shaped sound lens
                              focussing on footsteps tapping
In the chalk tabernacle
                stuffed with whispering pinions
                              in the rotundas
Angel-shapes, in every one
                a bird-winged Jesus-being
                              'knock and it shall…';
A gigantic duckchick
                crammed into its waters,
                              the murmuring shell,
The undercheep, faint
                underscratch, the mutter-egg,
                              strong ducks
Inside their seamless urns;
                mother and child peck in unison,
                              outside, inside;
The walls white as cliffs
                that pick and chirp,
                              the jagged plates loosen
And fall aside; his head

                        with a chick in it
                                    my chalky nails scratch
My skull of chalk;
                        chalky chicks, formerly eggs, their chirping
                                    overflows the river
In the stately wake
                        of the mother-chick
                                    formerly an egg;
The old powerhouse
                        littering its waste ground
                                    like a shattered egg,
The small flock glides past
                        in electrical sparks like sunshine
                                    learned in the Rotunda,
The round gallery, mother
                        with ah soft wings
                                    walking the round wall.

Seance for Fu-Manchu

The candle of Fu-Manchu
               the thunder of Fu-Manchu,
                             light one at the other,
Rainbow colours, each a different medicine;
                             the thunder followed him
Like a sky-high cape
               working and racking
                             the answers came to him
In the rain and from
               the chaos above
                             which had comments
On his every deed
               in Isla Nubla, Cloud Island, Isis Nubla
                             and Pieris-Butterfly:
By reflectance basking: they control
               the angle of the white portions
                             of their wings
That reflect back onto black
               heat-absorbing patches
                             close to the body:
Not only pattern
               but process as well; as Teredo rotates its shell drilling
                             into the sides of great ships or
Oxen haul 'logs over slick roads
                             greased with fish-oil' or
The medium hugs herself with happiness

                    to make the ghosts come
                                        opening and closing her wings
Like a mighty extra lung.

Ecophilia

Images wavering in the leaves
    trance-bearers
        pictures in the green fire
Green personages – dryads –
    painting the emerald –
        they have electropulse
And electrostatic,
    the magnets, the great ones,
        the natural condition is pulse,
Like the water shivering
    on each outstretched leaf,
        the natural condition is trance,
The hypnotism
    of the great trees gently swaying
        the breath coming off them
Full of suggestions;
    the art of love is hypnotism;
        surround the trance with enigmas
And it will strive to solve them;
    the green minister
        does not lift the curtain
On his own, or lift the green curtain
    by his efforts alone.

Painted in Apocrines

In the De Kooning show
                the paint from a special
                              oil selected by the artist
Smelt of women and that smell
                intermingled
                              with the aroma of the crowd;
The people are invisible landscapes
                painted in their apocrines,
                              their native body-lotions,
Their baby-lotions, 'synthesis of body,
                landscape and paint'; sexual intercourse
                              is coloured
Like De Kooning's pictures
                which are companioned by beings
                              of many odours;
This person sees itself
                in the pictures,
                              odorous self portraits;
This person steps
                out of the pictures
                              embraces me as an Arab would
With his exquisite painterly breath
                of the mad party in which
                              everybody exchanges rainbows
Like immense wings beating
                and the Star women covered in paint

					which leaps out
of its tin thirsting
				for the invisible to be
						made visible by pouring
Paint on the Bum;
				robing the scut
						with ineffable light.

Superwhite Extra-Large Perispirit

As I now beheld the shirt
                in cellophane, we were one
                              in the sameness of our forms
It became a mirror-image of myself
                I saw quiver over it
                              the crackling of a dry water:
I saw that it was about to speak,
                and I perceived the lightning static
                              which it nurtured in its weaves.
It hasteneth like knowledge
                from the hands of its bringers
                              so that I may expound it crisply
And deck myself with it
                and tune its buttons down my front
                              or wear it open to my breastbone
Gigantic labia,
                the air brushing at my
                              theatrical collar-bone
Like a radio set dialled to the aethyr
                or as though I had donned a sea-chart,
                              a treasure map with all its tidal openings;
And that water watched the skies above, and wove –
                my shirt studying with my skin
                              in their perispiritual tuning
Like surfs of echo of the secret world,
                like a trysting-tent inside the shirt,
                              like a tabernacle wedding-tent.

Invisible Until they Arrive

The great commissary-ships
                fed with the mists of forests
                              off-load into the large-windowed eateries
Unloading straight into the kitchens;
                you can watch as you feed,
                              how the stock flowing in from the seas
Never ceases or diminishes;
                still wheels of refrigerated mangoes
                              carried along the pier and up the hill;
Cunning plasms in painted pots,
                haunted patés and terrines,
                              a religious art that is edible;
The pious unpacking
                of solemn monstrances of small whales:
                              'See what you are going to eat'
Is the motto
                in the town's limitless dry sunlight
                              a real presence
That will not let you go.
                His diner's seat established here for ever
                              he returns never missing a main meal
To watching the ships as they ease
                on their tethers and reflections;
                              the red wines in dark tuns ready
To alter everything
                to arguments against leaving

                              before midnight or next year;
The town fed by the mists of forests
                    from which the white sails emerge
                              full-cargoed,
Invisible until they arrive.

Working the Chain

He would sit outdoors
                in all winds
                              al fresco in the waterhouse
Roofless observatory, working the chain,
                watching the county's maps
                              redrawing themselves
Across the sky,
                water picked up and shed everywhere,
                              arrested in reservoirs
And cisterns; he strikes
                the cistern with the lavatory-brush,
                              like a square drum,
Feels the landscape shiver inside
                the zinc tank above his head
                              where Hampshire pauses;
In the porcelain bowl
                his wee chimes like the sweet
                              cathedral bells of Canterbury
Having passed through
                all the churches and all the women
                              he having drowned his soft turds
In the water of the city of Hereford;
                now as he zips and leaves,
                              the kaolin-white of Cornwall
Assembled to hang above his head,
                freshening.

Amethyst Rock

'All the singing sands have a sparkling surface…',
New Scientist, 8 March 1997

A boulder of amethyst
        couches in its sands,
                arranges round itself
The locale named Rock,
        virtuosi arrive
                with lights, mirrors and meters,
The boulder shows them
        amethyst images
                of their procession
Advancing through fractures
        into the stone corridors,
                slipping
Through the silk rock…
        as the stones dwindle
                through the ages
New properties emerge
        music for instance;
                once there were
Only boulders littered
        where there are now
                flowing dunes;
The pebbles ground to sands
        sound a myriad hum
                that certain winds uncover;

Now one rock remains
        polished
                by its predecessor sands;
A hum of music and electricity
        generated by the chafing
                of gemstone fractal surfaces;
An electricity
        which slippers and hushes the feet;
            a spirit which gathers
In pools, each grain
        a maestro
                with his own pavilion of music;
Electrical hourglass;
        engine of innumerable
                cogs in one wheeling
Circuit; rocks
        that can pour and blow;
                rocks fluxile as water.

Woman Passing Through Book and Brick

'The transmigration of spirits as breaths…'
Gerald Massey, *The Natural Genesis*, p. 79

I.

It is partly bricks
              it is partly books
                                the distillery hidden
By the wall and the wall's
              inscriptions, it has
                                blocks of prose,
Stone verse with assonance,
              it is partly reader, partly writer
                                with quartz spectacles,
Sweating slightly as the story
              takes hold
                                and distilling in her breath
Her version of the story.

II.

That tail-coated maestro
              that cat like a black breath
                                allows his eyes to gold-blaze;
The can opens like a scroll
              to give him reeking cold fish
                                from seas of tin;
We learn our stretch and breath from him.

III.

Now the book begins to breathe,
                A cloud is emitted from the stone
                              and a corresponding fleece
Passes over Sagittarius,
                a heavy dew
                              falls on our shoulders
In the pattern of the set pieces
                of the constellations.

IV.

Now the book is charged
                can be put away for centuries
                              without the loss of its electricities,
The Laborator or Dealer
                adjusts the octavo distillery,
                              hides the book full of breath
In a wall of Reading Abbey;
                its elixir will pass through
                              all these walls
Whose stones will read it
                as per inscription, everlasting.

The Bed

The hare's marrow:
                the light of the moon;
                              the Big Dipper's mechanism:
Turn the earthly wheel
                sane energy gradually rises
                              as in a well-bucket,
A sacred marriage-scene
                engraved on the bucket
                              with dog under couch;
White light fills the bedroom,
                the great music house;
                              they who trill
Their voices in chanting
                enchant the feathers in the duvet
                              all beating at once.

Spiritualism Garden

Eating on the edge of death,
        the brink –
                green laburnum.
Black laburnum seed, the green forbidden
        the black full of power
                sharpening the presences
Of the garden by shifting of perception,
        the plants and trees
                offering their substances
To make their spirits visible
        in soft green seeds in rows
                which are death;
They must be dry and black
        rattling in the pods
                and I carried the black seeds about
In a white box
        which would tell me all
                from second month onwards
That happened beyond
        the portals of the worm
                to my siblings who were dead
Evolving into the apple-trees
        of Orchard End and its laburnums;
                I climbed up the laburnum ladder
For my lessons,
        I sat in a tree

                              eating the black seed of my siblings
Using their eyes
              to see the garden
                              with everything on the trembling
Edge of being seen, foetus, foetess,
              colloquy with my garden siblings,
                              green spiritualism;
The seasons change as I eat
              the black seeds, seeing.

Took Her for the Gardener

Bent over me
                       and kissed, saying
                                         she loved me;
Smelt sweet
                       and of the garden, flowers
                                         in beds, earth turned,
Open soil; she had been out
                       gardening, paused
                                         to kiss me, I could smell
The garden air speeding
                       over the rockeries;
                                       she is the gardeness…
Their prophet
                       was a carpenter,
                                       in the garden
Mistaken for a gardener;
                       there was a tomb in their garden
                                         smelling of nothing worse than garden,
Filled with spirit like the garden,
                       the rockery like a tomb broken open…
                                       she is going out to garden
Into a smell of rain and
                       turned earth, that sweetness
                                       swept out from the depths
And made a part of home and person.

Vine and Rain

New wine will rain
                from the mountains;
                              a mountain of wine
Changed from mountain to wine
                so we can drink mountain,
                              sing mountain,
Raising our glasses on the walkways
                through the vines, the fine
                              volcanic soil
Turning to grapes all around us...
                as volcano it is too heavy to hold;
                              as wine lift it and
It gives you added strength...
                a white ring-dove
                              alights on the telephone wires
Twined with messages like vines,
                              and the phone rings...
I take down
                the spiritual message, which is that
                              the gutters run with juice and that
Nothing will stop the volcanic
                mountain soil fermenting;
                              extract water from wine
And you have a volcano,
                and the volcano erupts grapes...
Also that pure water

      passes pontifflike through gutters
          in crystal white. So I drink up
This father-in-a-glass-of-water
     watching the mountain as I drink it up
        imbibing its waterfalls and cataracts
Hurrying through
     the busy vatican which is itself,
        sliding like a slim scabbard
Down the telephone wire…
     one palace run by a white father
       the other by a red one
Water and wine the two vaticans – one
    a lethargy maturing in the vineyard,
      the other
A sheer white exhilaration which
     will run anywhere if given the chance,
       picking up its white robes
And pouring down…
    how much should I drink?
       a sip, or as much as I could stand?
For I shall be water one day cascading
     down the mountain, or held
        for a sunshine caress in the vineyard –
Where I kiss the dusky tods of grapes…
     wine resting, water
       holding a service which sweetens it,
A church which is entirely juicy font,
    sapiens…

                                in St. Sapiens crypt creak
Its tuns like the ribs of giants
                quaffing themselves up
                                and accumulating in their souls
In exchange
                the natural spirit. This church
                                with a vineyard and a torrent grows
Its own wine from the dead returning,
                whose spirit is wine
                                which is the ghost of volcano –
Moves everywhere.

The Hotel and its Juices

There are small round tables
                and dove-breasted sofas
                              and a waiter skims
Through the clock large as a hotel;
                deep in its works
                              we wait time for our coffee;
My lover sips too
                from the black flower of the coffee-cup;
                              she sees syllogisms
In the wheel of odours
                as she tastes
                              the same black lotus;
We sip from its achieved blooms
                which are sweeted with enormous sugar
                              big as Chinese lanterns
Shedding their tasty light.
                (Doesn't the odour suddenly
                              appear everywhere like an apparition
With big sleeves?)
                The apparatus on its clockface tray
                              is a device
Of chrome and crushed beans,
                hot water, glass, filter-paper,
                              mainspring fragrance:
With invisible tendrils
                it is opening the mirrors.

                        Glitter appears,
Shining clockwork
          meshes around us,
                    time stops as the bitter black
Touches the palate-back
          where the secret fountains start.

The Arrival

So many of the walls
                depict robed guides:
                                figures painted in ores
And looming through the everwet
                walls; shining statues
                                upon whose heads
The waterfalls plash.
                For the humans
                                whose smoky lamps paint
Their ceilings in sfumage
                there are swifter guides,
                              wills-of-the-wisp
Skimming the surface of the
                underground lake
                              guide the penetrant oars
And there is slow lightning
                pointing the arches, electricity
                              from the dunes
Rolling overhead...
                there is an echo
                              like rubberlined doors
Squashily opening and closing, for
                there is a ceremony
                              hiding round every corner;
And there are pillars of limestone
                whose table-top is hollow

                                                            and contains
A serving of mud; collected for centuries,
                    small altars of mud
                                                so heavy it is pure; everything
Here weighs heavy with purity; the sand
                    underfoot drifts heavy
                                                because it is so pure,
Washed and rewashed
                    in the constant distillation
                                                of the cavern waters;
The air is heavier here
                    because of purity, and the great
                                                striding arches
Are pure in form because the water
                    has worn them that way.
                                                Close to these pedestals
In the presence of offered mud
                    the walls are more nearly
                                                transparent, and the guiding figures
Have approached nearer the surface,
                    nearer to stepping forward
                                                through the stone,
About to show their faces,
                    wiping away the limestone crusts,
                                                like rubbing sleepy-sand away
With the backs of their pebbled fists;
                                                a virgil has burst
Through the rock-grain with its scents and lotions;

     whomsoever it is, a presence
            passing through the Virgil Caves,
Passing through all the perfumes of Rock.

Astradame

I.

Each act of love
                adds an extension to our home
                              our Astradame
The tremulous arrival of
                our joined word
                              into the moonspace, dunespace;
Huge banks of fog-silence gliding
                like liners carved out of cloud
                              packed with thunder-passengers
Steadying into a silence
                the interval
                              between one dune and another:
We walk together through the dunes
                a kind of people who shake silence
                              'with great vigour behind the scenes'
A sack of warehouse spices employed as the bed.

II.

The fog moves in
                with chilly haste,
                            the offices, warehouses, docks
Lose their particular dimension,
                the people of them
                              lose their usual feel:

Instead it is
                  The House of the Hushed Beard,
                              I am tangled in the Father's beard.
It is very quiet in here, and deaf.
                  How will he speak next?
                              By what means
Pronounce his next Cabbalah?

Door Among the Dunes

St. Enodoc

Over and over, the same face
                      in variable whispers, the face
                                      that watches the sandbound
Church from all sides;
                      the dunes nudging the church
                                    flowing over the church
Concealing and revealing it,
                      reproducing the
                                    countenance of the wind;
The square entrance
                      among sliding dunes;
                                    the whole summer stained
With quiet thunder of the dunes…
                      he entered the sandgrain
                                    entered the sand-dunes,
Taking them to be
                      of the church equally:
                                  he entered the sand-dunes
In a million persons;
                      and he comes in from the sandgrains
                                  he arrives driving the chariot
Of each sandgrain, of all the sandgrains;
                      he unties the braids of his sandy beard
                                  unrolls it down to his feet,
It fills the church,

                        pours over the altar;
                                        then the wind blew
And he picked up
                        his countenance again
                                        from the dunes,
And walked into the stone
                        of the church, into
                                        the single great sandgrain
Of the church;
                        the magical sand
                                        radiating quiet ghost
Sharing it with the sun
                        in a million persons
                                        opening the sand-doors,
Church turning to dune,
                        dune to church.

Resin

His walkman speaking into him
                two bees tugging and squeaking
                              at the flowers of his ears
The shoals of herring
                the schools of whales that pull
                              across the harbour water
In oily sperm
                in rainbows of it and clotted butterpats;
                              dews of the women,
Resins of them:
                it was the gardening
                              she had not yet done
But planned to do before tea, perfumed her
                as the weather does –
                              flowers alter time;
A man cycling, carrying daffodils
                in the crook of his arm.
                              The flowers
Like see-through sails
                fan out their scent
                              as he pedals emitting
A full-rigged ghostyacht
                in a squall of scent
                              changing the scale of events,
Reaching on the port tack,
                shivering and reaching, steered
                              by Walkman.

Bearded Gold

The mineral train rushing by
>> truck-full of bright white sand
>>>> and tawny gravel,
The music of the pieces
>> clashing together,
>>>> the bounding boulders,
The glassy sandgrains
>> like innumerable lanterns,
>>>> heavenly mansions:
In this train I am able to visit
>> my spring self; that day
>>>> I had no soul so I borrowed one,
It looked like a mineral train,
>> a golden beard, each spasm
>>>> gave a little cry,
The golden hair
>> rushing under the bridge;
>>>> I tested my condition
Of trance by breathing
>> into my beard, gold metal
>>>> that is not dark
Not even inside itself;
>> or I could offer
>>>> a beardless gender
If I wanted to converse
>> fearlessly with ghosts; many

                              have misinterpreted
The monk's cowl, hooded,
              for a haunted ballroom gown; so, descending,
                          I lighted her bearded
Lantern, she trimmed
              my flame for me; it was a house
                          full of lighted lamps, where she
Poured her gold
              into my crucible that
                          rushed through
Like a mineral soul of goldglass
              travelling on our behalf, metal
                          visiting our springselves.

Fey Body

In counterchanging velvet dress
        every movement a scudding patch,
                slows light down, looking
Wet and dry at once
        like rumours of alchemical water;
                creases, beams scurry
In mud of light
        scrying in the skin-dress
                soft pulses over wholeskin
Darkening with patches
        clear again,
                rhythm woven over the down,
A raster of touchsight;
        by her amazed smile
                she knows
The sea-kelpie tribe,
        is ready to leave the skin
                of slither on it again
Like a garment of knowledge,
        fey skin, foetal,
                fleeced with lanugo
Light-speaking frock
        alphabet of shining
                where cunning lingers.

Fall Graduate

The Fall Graduate of Canned Beer
                visits the Islands;
                              the mothy gates
And fanning doors,
                the winged gateways
                              of headhigh grasses;
Doves bob
                dipping into the nightdew
                              with boozy bosoms
Like old ships' figureheads;
                rough-hewn moontemples,
                              settled boulders,
Moonbeam rafters,
                rude granite rooflessnesses;
                              I fill my pewter
With the beer from cans,
                the feathery foam
                              pouting rises
Like the breast of a dove;
                its stardome bubbles
                              coo a round astonished hiss;
The violin-brown beer-orchestra
                intoxicates and connects him
                              with the naked ceiling of stars,
He crisp-pisses the sparking domes about
                converting booze into an ancient song,

                                    opening his doors,
Dashing immemorial urine down
                on immemorial stone.

Head Door

I.

Pillows painted with pictures;
        further worlds slipping
                through a small torn
Door in the bolster;
        a little Jesus
                darts out of the
Sleeping skull, slips
        into the feather-land
                full of beating wings;
It is the Jesus of him,
        the sleeping-self,
                the head door in
The portals of the brain,
        wearing your wings
                beyond the pillow,
The feathers stuffed
        with gull-cries and
                incipient angels
Of the dream which follows the
        interpretation, always.

II.

I took my dream
        to 24 interpreters in Falmouth;

				all gave different

Interpretations;
				all were fulfilled.

The Teaching

A gentleman might build
                an echo in his park
                              tuned according to the
Time of day and the air's
                elasticity. Dry light
                              is best.
Authentic, and living on a pill? No, rather
                'the demi-genius bestowed
                              upon him by the sky…'
A rapture discovers itself; source of depression
                in failure of recollection, say; say
                              a prebirth liquid garment
Fashioned in the palace laboratory; the tree
                of the placenta in human form
                              conducting them through
The forest; leaf-coloured eyes,
                leaf smell that clings in the clothes,
                              the movements of liquid
In their sacs before the rain;
                the schoolmasters admit that their persons
                              were their knowledge,
The coming and going of realisation-smells
                the gift of a good teacher, modulated
                              by pipe and tweeds which are
Warm and magnetised into answers;
                              see the Independent article

On the schoolgirls who learned their piece
               in the presence of a chosen smell.
                             recalling their subject-matter
In the exam-room by virtue
               of that same smell of the teaching;
                             graduating: chasing
That evening fireflies in the late
               coolness; no candidate bruised
                             by her ordeal-smell.

From His Time Machine

He undid a lingham
                from his time machine scripture
                              a little engine
In a beautiful cabinet;
                time-travelling by notebook.
                              He time-travels
To the end of his sentence,
                the right-hand of his signature
                              flies up,
It is like a crack in the paper
                he has to end-stop
                              to prevent it flying away:
The whole book, please
                shake it a little –
                              it rearranges and crystallises
Itself; it is a laundry of the patriarchs
                that cleans the mourning clothes
                              and sews the ripped
Rich garments into many varnished
                buttons and versicles
                              made visible at last, at least.

Poems Found in Commonplace Book

Her lopsided mouth
                gave the widow 'great beauty and stealth'
                              in the congregation of 'Big Shoulders'
Where 'the gassy gunpowdery smell
                of human winds'
                              blew, church-shaped smoke
Settling for a moment
                the smell of dead flowers
                              and alcohol and
Cinnamon in the embalming fluid,
                made the corpse
                              smell like a flower
In a forest of big-shouldered coffins,
                I rap on the foot,
                              of my father's box,
And weep; his shadow
                is a magnet, his bone-dome
                              becomes an oneirogrome

Occupied by the hanging road,
                the Milky Way, and here down below
                              a necrospasm or turbine, self-generating
Depression called
                The Crime at Vlad's Cape, who left
                              the needle in from the veiled
Spirit-world that pricks everyone

                    who tries to pick it up, called also
                                riding the corkscrew or dad's death
For long after he had left
                the light in death's house burned on
                              with a nameless colour, such as you see
On the necks of turtle doves: milky grey.

Cabala Mount

The mountain breathes
                through its many beards
                              it is 75% beard
Beard-hair and stubbled rock
                gorse bristle-haired
                              it is one of the churches
Of water and grey rock and whiskers
                and the clouds
                              rising and falling therein
Inside as well as outside
                changing the mountain's wind-pitch,
                              there are tubes that are rivers
And tubes finer than human-hairs,
                from mine-shudders sounding to piccolo-notes
                              over under-estuaries
And lakes dark as stout,
                darkness full of white beard,
                              extra beards
Spun by spiders and by briars
                beard transmitted through the rocks
                              where rock lays down the throne it builds
Throne of beards
                great beard spilling with its juices
                              among inner air softer than beards,
Beards that pulse as if speaking
                beards that speak without moving;

                                      cavemen have drawn in
The great ruffles of beard on the mystery-walls;
                we must wear beards to enter,
                          oh but it is hair,
Women's hair:
                those great volutes are moon-rock
                      moon-face,
The great grey hair that tunnels the unshaven rock.

Caverns and Towers

A rough road winding
>> to and fro between
>>>> conical turfy hills that are
Quarry-snot and grassy spoil;
>> a rubbled, hazardous post-industrial
>>>> road serving
The dynamited cliffs – they are always
>> opening and delving
>>>> with pick and explosive
Further caverns
>> and caverns containing caverns
>>>> under caverns
As if the origin
>> of the world were caverns.
>>>> The cliffs spoil,
Make hillocks knotted together
>> by seeding speeding grass.
>>>> Some homes are built
Up against the rockface
>> which is delved full of castles
>>>> and limestone naves
And unexpected entrances, this linen cupboard
>> a deep shaft among the shirts;
In one of the larger caves
>> the main trusses are framed
>>>> with arched braces and collars

And enriched with stone flowers
                        and stalactites where chiming water
                                            continues her work,
Of falling and rounding.
                        The mistress of the place
                                        came into the house
Out of the wet cave behind it,
                        smelling like a woollen flower;
                                        on the thirtieth day of her cycle
In my sleep
                        a wide shaft opened in the ground
                                        like Tretower Castle reversed
And I fell.
                        When I woke
                                        after falling for ever
It was on the cliffs
                        the valleys spread out
                                        so high up
It felt still like deep down;
                        there were percussive
                                        faint hammer-blows
In the cliff face behind me,
                        the abrupt song
                                        building more houses in houses
Hammering in the caverns
                        the working song.

Blue Cricket

Childhood dream
                of my face in the Moon
                              and my black beret
The earth's slant shadow
                straightens the woodland path
                              in order to molest
The ancient dragon
                who breathes out
                              the northern lights
The breath of which
                scorches the forest in autumn;
                              the dew which is medicine
Settles on the cupolas of acorns
                of the president oak;
                              with a slightly-trained eye
A Westerner can discern
                dragons in the landscape,
                              the White Worm of Whitehall,
A civil servant can…
                the rooms gathered
                              an atmosphere of bad joss
Like grey dragons becoming still
                and pretty as savoy
                              or elaborate castled
Patties, or pagodas, replicas
                of a balanced universe

                                        light playing about the roof
Like a blue cricket-game,
              the snick of electricity,
                           the leisurely blue figures,
Lightning fondling the House,
              Big Ben with his beret
                           half on; the secret
Of the silver and the gold
              is a dark garment
                           and sponge-bag trousers
And a City voice: it is the visit
              of a demon if you feel sick
                           afterwards; an angel
If you feel good; or both at once
              when it is a daemon; but
                           if there is depression
Say: 'We can mine here' starting
              when the clock stops and the dragons
                           will assist
If you are sincere
              and trust their flames; voting
                           with their flames.

The Font

She was from her belly and had made
A divine shape in it, as

The horse stamps rainbows
Out of the wet earth.

A font installed this morning in the church:
All the water in the world,

The cliff of the cold front
Pouring with waterfalls,

Passes through the human keyhole.
I had you by air and fire,

In vital atmosphere,
Wildfire-wet,

A small black bird
In the hand beating-wet.

Solid Prayers

Sex as solid prayers
               full of stars!
                             a high degree of reality
In the starry turning dome-stage where
               she struts her funky stuff,
                             rain, skin and sweating slightly
To shine, making
               a heiroglyph with each
                             ritual unconscious gesture
Saying
               I am here
                             I am here again
I am here still,
               I am here there everywhere;
                             she turns up her shine
Of the three colours which are gates:
               black oral, white smile,
                             rouge lips; also
I know her from her gait
               which struts
                             marching astride
Her pelvic cask,
               she swings on her gates
                             everlastingly, all smile
Her smile everywhere
               the barrel full of womanly ale,

                              hale and bellowing like a whale

As she blows and puts her tongue out
              meaning

                              I can fellate you with this.

In the Year of the Comet

The roads are long metallic
                rays of stars,
                              the comet is a great
Frozen lake flying in the sky, vibrating
                reeds, ice-waterfalls and all,
                              a lake of frozen pitch flying,
A salt marsh flying;
                a thunderclap from the blowhole;
                              the spray flies up in a cloud
in which a rainbow hovers
                like a comet's trail
                              we are passing through,
An entrance to the comet
                in seven colours, thundering;
                              that winter
We cut steps in the gigantic ice
                and went in and out of the house
                              by the lavatory window,
Cut steps and paths
                in the frozen pitch
                              and in the saltmarsh:
Our upstairs room
                was called the Gynoecium
                              because it was hers,
And she cleaned its wide-curving windows
                so we could look out

                                    while we were in bed
In the comet's spectrum halls.

The Boys Inside the Hills

(Ritual from the Stone Age)

Each hill is horn-hollow; musically,
                The agreeable humiliation of a slippery sinkhole
                              is your introit,
On your bottom you slide
                into the protocathedral choir,
                              in sturdy boilersuits
You rummage yourself into the mud,
                you worm through a mere crack
                              into the hill's
Cathedral chamber-arch;
                You are 'Kepyr,
                              the type of transformation
By rolling round and round',
                you are one
                              with the immense flesh of mud,
In the floppy corpses of your overalls,
                dressed in corpse to pass through corpse;
                            Kevin Kephyr
Lights an oily rag
                flings it out over the water
                            where it floats scudding
Like a soul-boat
                pulling out from the pillars
                            and underlit chancellaries
Their shadows

                    in systole packed into dark patches
                                in diasatole
A Palm Court again…
                    now the tadpole black adventurers
                                plying their mucky hands
Whistle and trumpet down the main chambers,
                                bellow down the sidechapels,
Into the sidechambers
                    to arouse as they did
                                the shadows,
The black echoes through the mountain shafts:
                    mountains below, hills above, singing a while
                                with the boys who
Thrust themselves back
                    into the sunshine
                                as from a mother.

Library Lab

I.

The tree – they 'wove hangings
               and covered it with their broidered
                             garments', dressed it up
Like a woman; under her skirts:
               forests. The conjurer
                             disappearing his lady
And reappearing her
               in timber cabinets,
                             under table-cloths
Is discovering anima mundi
               everywhere: I am,
                             I am here, everywhere;
Now any empty space
               could be her or in her.

II.

Ora et labora; alchemist,
               in the library which is his laboratory,
                             sets up his pipes, tubes and globes,
A laboratory shining with its glasses
               that are books so excited
                             that they start to distil their contents
Not waiting
               to be warmed by the reader's eyes.

III.

Prayer, ora, is transformation of ores.
>> By praying the alchemist enters
>> >> a dowsing condition,
His retorts
>> sigilise sexual intercourse,
>> >> he is now a Detector and Inspector
Of the minute electricities
>> that prickle over the rock samples.
>> >> The vapours speak to him
As they enter him,
>> the word 'metal' in Langland
>> >> means 'dream', opening thus
The planetary gates in the operator,
>> his flowering wheels, his faire fields.

IV.

These practices
>> touch the hem of the spirit
>> >> abroad in the air
Prickling like starlight,
>> elastic air which is also
>> >> the quickening sexuality
Of the alchemist's delight
>> and bliss as he kisses
>> >> that hem again;
This spirit is vulva-hemmed.

Unpredictable Acoustic

Ship of cats;
                 a skiff of dogs drifts by
                               the volume turned up;
Streets of the rivers
                 named after lovers,
                               the boy sleeping
In the longboat of radishes.
                 Is Arthur returned?
                               he will get a job
As highdiver with the circus;
                 the silvering dawn
                               heirlooms the city with ice,

A strange unpredictable acoustic
                 travelling with the fullmoonlight:
                               she dreams that her true name, Arthur
Appears in big golden letters
                 studded over the full moon…

She gets a high-diver job in the circus
                 and will wear tights
                               spangled with little lights
Spelling out Arthur
                 to enter the water,
                               and a job
Grafting pears in the forenoon.

Henrhyd Waterfall

Is like the bow window
                of an ancient ship
                              sunk in its vale;
In this drought
                only a little flow
                              tumbles into the air
Off the high lip of rock
                and the captain's
                              stateroom windows are
Blind stone. There is still
                a hint of rainbow
                              in the gulf
A rainbow scent
                or sensation in the
                              presence of the cliff
Which at spate cascades
                bending its stout rainbow
                              in mid-air
Like the shining mainspring
                in a clock
                              of seven colours
Its tensions
                demonstrated
                              by its colours;
But today you see
                the fall's foundation

                              of rock, the dry
Nether underpinning
                of the famous rainbow.
                                The Fall
Has followed us home
                and the boulders abound,
                                and the stone of the hotel
Walls seem underpinning
                for rainbows; a fly
                                from the falls
Hanging suddenly on the clear
                outside bedroom window glass
                                seems a seed of that water's
Withdrawn force, a seed
                of that water's force;
                                it lands straddled on the glass
Flexing its rainbow waxes
                like a black star
                                with its legs stretched
A visitor of the black underground water
                                and its batwings
Like a draughtsman's
                perfect equilibrium
                                of flying forces, like a
Denotation water
                captured and controlled
                                in an insect virility;
One of the thirsty parched mariners

                that glide through the stone fissures
                            powered by secret rainbows,
The colours on the air
        of the speed
                    of the ship's still wake
at Henrhyd Falls.

On the Links

Golfing in sea-fog and fog-horn
                stimied by all the bushes
                              Calendar House with its rain-guages
The moon in the storm-rack,
                dragons fighting over a huge, pocked pearl
                              driven into the rough
The 365 windows staring out to sea
                the engulfing mist rising from the sea-gulf
                              satellite pictures of England
Entering the great wheel of mist,
                her liquid mirror
                              her shining furrow or track
Moon-track clearing
                a hole-in-one
                              her cushioned interior
Like a royal train
                all plush and buttoning;
                              she stretched her prune
Down over me,
                her left breast tasted salt,
                              her right, of honey,
The moon lost among the bushes and bunkers
                and found again,
                              the star-jasmine
Mistressed the night,
                her dress mingling with the bush

                              or was it her perfume
From her ripening diamond
                as we washed ourselves
                                with pads of the misty moss
We felt tall as the moon-filled sky
                then on to fish
                                and clear white wine:
The communion meal of the ocean,
                at home on the links
                                among the correspondences.

Dante by the Seaside

Purgatory Tower

I.
The earth like a friend
                who changes her perfume
                              according to the seasons
And her needs.
                The muted unending lighting
                              in the pearly clouds
Of February – we live rubbed
                between endless sheets
                              of slow lightning:
They coil like the purgatorial spirals
                of Dante, and as if to confirm this
                              they have built us a conical
Truncated black glass tower
                for a swimming-pool that
                              emulates a lower cornice of Purgatory.
This tower of ours
                models the invisible lightning of the place,
                              it is smooth and transparent
As a waterfall over black rock,
                it is the portal out of which
                              ghost pours into the land
In the form of refreshed swimmers
                and in other two-legged creatures
                              stepping into the branchline train

From which we see the black portal
                hanging in the blue sky:
                              the veritable end of the line:
A black frustrum
                hanging in the blue,
                              like a caisson,
Like the stilled plinth of a tornado
                full of everything, though
                              as an entertainment facility,
It encloses Spring all the year round
                in a garden at the heart of the mountain
                              of erotic lightning
(A subtle form of rain) of the boom
                of divers calling in the truncated
                              thundercloud, containing
Waterfalls flume-filled with swimmers, while
                being black, it depicts Eros,
                              the painter in all colours.

II.

It is our spaceman's monolith
                of which they cry out
                              'But it is full of stars!'
At night you can see right down
                to the glowing heart-pool of the hill.
                              In daytime it is bible-hued
Glass in which hangs by black mirror

      the whole town of 25,000 souls;
        house of fire by night.
It is also a slow-orgasm machine:
      plunge into the water –
        it unifies the skin
Whose many silky pages are windows
      opening wide, the orgasm of the town
        is pooled among the swimmers
In big waves rocking
      in their still cradle:
        electrical water
Being total skin, shared; to perform
      the backstroke under the glass
        hatchways to the stars;
Like the pied hill opening in Hamlyn;
      Persephone water, dark and light;
        chimney-stack pulling to the underworld;
The renewed sinner-swimmers trooping out,
      their towels like much-read
        library loans,
Soaked with feeling, tucked
      under their arms
        (to go down
Into the dark water
      and return far better than before).

The Index

Walking with electrical legs
         in noisy nylons
                 electrical dress;
The blackberry bush
         shining in the sunlight
                 like a great cinema organ
Rising up in the season;
         their clothes blowing
                 in a wind that doesn't touch us;
The house with the books
         in itself sealed writing;
                 he is turning to spirit
So he can enter the house
         and the books in the house
                 and the powers inside the books
Sending out their nature again
         like the obverse spider
                 dazzles, with scudding
Soap-bubbles blows out,
         blows out the old flies
                 dazzling us with
The years of flies-made-again,
         backwards flying;
                 and the hum of flies courting
The egg in the cherry;
         the table spread with cherries,
                 the spider kneeling

And blowing out its flies,
        blowing its groceries,
                backwards trees sucking –
In their first fruit;
        the dead folk
                reform underground
Like potatoes, are dug up,
        brushed off, bathed,
                and that is where
Babies come from,
        the potato-beds; he looks up
                out of his book where
Spiders are indexed, and ripe cherries,
                cadavers and gritty spuds
And the hum of flies,
        and three circles,
                two reflecting each other
And the third a shining fire
        shining equally from the other two,
                a direct glance
Which waxes to a gaze
        entitled how
                to make eye-contact during
Lovemaking: one self looking through
        both pairs of eyes, a double one-ness,
                the book called Suitemate,
Bound in one volume
        the scattered leaves.

Comestible Orchestra

The waiters snake in
        like willowy water;
                the diners stab their steaks
Or call for services;
        the music owns the restaurant
                and the diners,
The musac plays non sequiturs
        in reverse heartbeat,
                the music conducts
The diners' hungers:
        they eat intently to the violin solo
                the music owns the restaurant
And the diners,
        with the first forkfuls that pass
                the lips; all
Utensils are put down gently
        as the music softens;
                they twirl their tulip glasses
Like ears of wine,
        they masticate intently
                to the violin solos,
By listening in time to
        the owner's radio station.
                The waiters execute
A watery step-and-glide;
        the music owns the restaurant and all utensils,

                                        the glasses, bowls, dishes,
Cups and saucers, built for resonance
                                        with the Patron's favourite tunes;
They eat intently off them
                to the violin solo
                                        and they ring softly
To a vocalist's distant passion;
                more food ladled on the plate
                                        mutes the buzzing china
And shivering knives, but the diners
                scrape their bowls restoring harmony;
                                        the diners book their usual places
Consulting the broadcasting-music schedules
                                        and the violin sonatas –
Hush! the soup-song is
                fading from the palate,
                                        gathering in the dishes:
Tinkle with your spoons
                to wake the willowy waiters
                                        who serve the gateau
Sonata in strict tempo;
                the diners are eating up
                                        to hear more clearly
The music which owns
                the Patron and the diners,
                                        they eat intently to the violin solos.

Scene Shifting

The body of the train
                is clothed still with her scent,
                              the ticket-collector
Under the dark of his peak
                smiles like a museum guard,
                              ushers us into a time train;
The railway guard operates
                a moving village
                              with periodic stops in town
And countryside, the railway connector,
                              the train fitting the platform,
The platform in intercourse with the train,
                              a whistle blows and the ghost passes,
The people pass like ghosts to their destination,
                the train withdraws
                              and proceeds, satisfied,
Throwing its golden panels of light
                on to the snow-banks it travels through;
                              a town that stops at the Dell.
Even the smaller trains are great houses
                full of scenery, framed, cross between
                              cinema, museum, theatre
Seldom less than three storeys long
                never a bungalow, the windows
                              packed with fluid geography.
I hope the guard always has as good dreams;

      the towns connected by the rails
          along which long beings shunt…
Reading the windows of these great books,
    easy journey.

I Was Myself Again

First I saw only the cafe,
        then I saw
                the dolomite in which the cafe
Was set, and I was myself again; the women
        gone off to Plymouth,
                on the waters;
Thank you for not smiling
        in this area
                where they say farewell
Watching the castle floodlit
        on its dolomite
                retreating with the bay.
The lost statues on the lost paths,
        the statues as the day advances
                grow warm as flesh, at night
Cold as rivers and fetters,
        but she is herself again;
                she sleeps among the stacks
Of frames carved into the shapes of angelwings waiting
        for their personages to don them, to put on
                harmony in the harp factory;
Another of her gifts
        'was the imparting of sweet perfume
                to those she touched' –
The bodies that served them well
        as trysting places, and would once more
                as she was herself again.

The Handclasp

Shaking hands with the dead man
                who is no millionaire
                              Langland remarks
That it is the rich men
                who putrefy in the tomb,
                              but for the poor man
Who is dry, the earth
                is his laboratory and in the
                              contemplation of it he
Distils his aethyrs; that is
                he converts himself by study to travelling
                              charged vapours by the distillations
Of his bones, the leather bottles
                of guts and brains, the duple retort
                              of his nostrils and eyesockets,
Thus he projects
                a fair likeness of spirit-stuff
                              that we can almost see
And we get a whiff
                of the purified corpse
                              that is the condensation
Of himself and more personal
                than bones. So we greet
                              one another, I as towards
A perfected master – we clasp hands firmly,
                              his touch refreshes,

It is cool to my hand like
                the passing of a ghost or a mood
                              or an aethyr –
The poor man gone
                is converted to a mood
                            that will return
When either of us need it, the alchemist
                underground who can ride the wind,
                            greeting his fellow-students;
Dr. Plowman says, after Yeats:
                'these moods
                            are the Labourers and Messengers
Of the ruler of All-Living;
                immortal moods…'

Lizard Moonscape

Lizard lighthouse and lighthouse-buildings,
                cottages of the moon,
                              towers of the moon,
Moon beam towers in its orbit
                shining with moon-substance,
                              window moongloss,
Moonwish, moonwash,
                calcamine of the moon
                              moon-chimneys smoking
Like meteor-craters
                jet black or all white
                              the tower piled inside
With brass instruments, up to the
                cyclopean eye
                              like a whole brass band
Crammed into a moontower
                for creating orbital beams
                              that guide the ships home,
Scientific trombones and tuning lanterns
                playing the protective lightbeams
                              a safety melody rondo presto,
My friend in charge of light
                climbs his spiral stairs in his dressing-gown
                              hums a safety melody on his way
To bed, the safest bed in all the kingdom.

Observatory

As the moon rose in a sequence
                of venerable grey rainbows
                              the rain skidded
In white pulses over the cupola,
                the celebrated cupola of the marriage;
                              the spraying tyres
Of weather-cyclists;
                we penetrated numberless veils,
                              the moon's light alive
In every drop of the rain
                condensed on the cupola
                              and its matter guttering;
The moonlight spread everywhere,
                blowing in its veils,
                              a beam striking each drop
(All was illustrative
                of the wedding-veil)
                              wet as the bride veiled
Rainy in her sopping dress
                in the cupola of her skirts
                              or is that the moon,
The cupola, or her haunting dress
                that moves through the rainy
                              forest, at the moon's wheel-will
Or the cupola like a travelling fountain
                in the rainy forest

                                    approaching the cupola
To be married to the fixed smell
                whose cupola is it which opens,
                                so it is hers, with all its moisture,
And rain dashes across it,
                call it the master-bedroom
                                but it is the bridal-drone
Who lies in the bed
                and watches the rain washing
                                over the leaden dome
Which opens to the moonlight and the rain
                where she lies on the bed
                                opened by the moon,
Opened by the forest, the rain, cupola, self –
                her cupola opening – she is in all these places
                        at once.

Books and Vistas

I.

At the Round Ponds
        the fishes going
                round and round
Like a perfect water-clock
        the golden fish
                and the silver ones
Denoting the surrounding lands
        rich on gold and tin
                as if the ores swam
In the form of the fish
        and the light crackles and flashes
                on the fishbacks
Like a firmament
        of constellations spinning
                in subterranean flocks.

II.

He converts the bullet-hole into
        a buttonhole
                on his way to church;
He has been shot but the blood
        has become flowers
                and he's walking steadily;
The blood now flower

has become an independent
oracle, carried into a pew.
He bends the flower to his nostril
it is praying, he whispers
I can smell it praying,
I will pray as the flower in my lapel
prays, it shows me
how
Lodged in his left lapel
over his heart,
warmed by his chest
It emits its heart-perfume
filling the nave
like the breath in the stone
Flowering.

III.
The book as mask, but first
the book as trysting-place:
enter its 200 doors,
It lies wide open on his desk
its presence guarantees meaning
like a woman's lap,
The legs which are the pages open
and it speaks from down below
where the author loud
And silently narrates;

                    if you will bend to the shelves
                                    you will hear the best
New books speak and read the older books
                    in their leather jerkins
                                    The covers have grown
Their own designs, guiding by feel
                    and fragrance; if you will,
                                    pluck the book
Out of the gardens of reading
                    pages also like flowers;
                                    handle the understood book,
Light pours out of its pages;
                    take down that big house
                                    of many roofs tiled with utterance
And echoes of all previous books
                    via metaphors and alphabet because
                                    each letter is gendered,
Each word gendered,
                    gender into speech
                                    which is gendered
In a macho leather jacket, shining black,
                    in a soft suede waistcoat
                                    pockets full of characters
And the face it was written with,
                    the masks ranked in shelves
                                    you put on a new book
As you read it again.

Prince Plum's Furniture

Removing the great halls piecemeal,
                dust by dust which is the furniture
                               a great hall on the pattern
Of the chrysalis, it is an insect temple
                for calling up the insect powers
                               its humming vibrant plates
Inscribed with insect scores
                for you to sing, and grow wings,
                               the tin singing, the use
Of its plaintive cry, brings
                the moths in – and danger!
                               a dragon in the garden
As soon as she lights the bonfire
                its mane the big lion partnerships
                               and pastures of Prince Plum
A face whose smiles
                have been worked on by the sky;
                               my glasses, quietly dreaming
With a dragon roaring in the chimney-schloss
                inventing the snowstop to protect
                               the moths
A square day like a stroke of luck
                like a furnace door swinging open
                               ringing as a cathedral bell
A dragon from the atlas
                becoming a woman, before my time,

                        a furnace opened
Freely entered, and left, singing of moths:
            In gratitude to Prince Plum
                        who shrivels off his stone at last.

Sweetness of Light

To sit down at one's meals
>>as the bee
>>>>settles to its flower,
Among its corridors of gloss,
>>mildness of temper
>>>>sweetness and light:
Honey and wax;
>>painting the house with gloss paints
>>>>so it resembles
The interior of a flower
>>fluorescent beehouse
>>>>beeflower
Flowerbee, fitting the flower-mask on;
>>their mildness
>>>>of table-manners
The bowed head incorporating
>>knife and fork,
>>>>the floury beard shared
With home bees, foreign bees,
>>with bees of all nations;
>>>>the thick-piled
Flying carpet of the hive
>>tuned like an organ
>>>>with a business-beenote,
Busy with clean air
>>in clean wings

                                        in a waxy clean light,
With a clean sound
                    in the fertility churches
                                    (all belfry)
Worshippers swarm
                    each after their pollen-crust
                                    the winding air-borne procession
To the egg of the flower,
                    musical pistil, pollen-torch
                                    shaking flame through
The rainbow corridors
                    to taste
                                    saliva at the altar,
To taste amaroli
                    to taste cunni
                                    like good malt whisky
Everybody by the ceremony
                    tastes their balsams gladly
                                    all the mouths
Become one mouth
                    to taste with one's inner
                                    distilling sheds
To taste inwardly
                    as the bee of oneself
                                    the spirit
Sipping deep
                    within the face.

Three Bells

The chime of a bell
     from somewhere in the front of the house
         as along a corridor
Which did not exist. I responded
     by shaking the Piskie Bell on my desk.
         I had tied red ribbons
Like a sash of honour round the torso
     which was also the handle of the bell,
         and round the small chain
Which was the clapper,
     to prevent inadvertent
         and unattended chiming.
The latter I untied
     and chimed back
         to the mystery bell.
The Piskie tone was clear and sweet
     and deepened as I brought it near
         the Singing Bowl I had chafed
With its wooden stick to bring forth
     its seven-metal tone.
         It was thus I answered the mystery-bell
With two mystery-bells of my own:
     a Piskie-bell and a sonorous Bowl;
         it was like a sounding
Liquid round Bell and Bowl
     pouring into each other,

                              calling out to each other
And to the sourceless note
                  that called them
                              as from a garden at the end
Of the non-existent corridor
                  a door half-ajar and the note
                              arising from somewhere
In the garden;we were joined
                  into the unity of volume:
                              Bell-tone fills room,
Body, estuary; the Piskie
                  in her Shiva-pose with her heel
                              stopping her cuntanus,
Sounding in answer to the seven stars
                  or metals, the weather full
                              of secret doors made of rain
Turned into music, trio
                  of the rainy garden, answering my
                              need for mystery.

Portals

I.

The water darkens before
The grey clouds, light
At the bottom of the garden
Is bent double, folded
Like a lens magnifying
Ships on the lake;

Cloud-shadow strides
Down over the yellow hill-fields
With rapid, concise, large
Movements. The lake's edge
Intervenes and the vast shadows become
Evenly spread in its roughened surface,

And darken there, in deeper shadows,
Even before the sky truly darkness.

II.

They are like Arabian carpets
Travelling under a spell

Both above the ocean
And within it,

Fleets of speedy
Arabian medusae. Despite
All this darkness
Arranging itself
Piecemeal in lake and sky
The sun is a mirror on fire
Hollowing out shapes with its shadows,

With slant shadows of the rocks
Creating every kind of doorway,
Portal, threshold, boundary, slant lintel
And domain.

Passing Clouds

A cloud haunting a big tree
                turning it white
                              with its water-load:
The cloud under the trees
                a static or slow fountain
                              taking shelter from
The slope of rain
                the slantwise of it;
                              water so we can see
And moisten our tongues
                so we can speak
                              of the tree
Full of stilled water...
                Read the fatrolls of cloud
                              as rainsources,
Or as shooting pains
                in my shoulder like lightning
                              in the joints, like flints
Struck together in constellations;
                read as an energy-shadow,
                              another self arriving
As a black mood
                which lightens as the rain busts
                              its cloud...
Electrical weather
                like a Frankenstein garden

          brings the disturbed scientist
Out to his laboratory of roomy clouds,
    he is like a vibrant spark
          like the other vibrant sparks
in his machinery darting
      from demonstration to demonstration…
          First the weather
Builds the laboratory
     which assembles its switchboards
         that then mould Frankenstein
Who stitches his Monster together,
     coils blooming in
         long sparks, terminals
Blazing like Xmas trees…
     The weather enrages him
         the weather wants his rage,
Rain-rage, thunder-rage
     which it exchanges for electricity
         that is blood of the Monster
And shining bones
     and studs in the neck
         and shuffling size fourteens…
And how does the Monster fare?
     he is settled weather itself
         something has been created
Brought down
     into this castle and garden,
         and the human rain-shadows

Called moods fly to and fro chattering
               tended by Him
                                      as a friend of the sky.
The weather's rages pass over him
               he pulls down his thunderhat
                             over his brows,
He is radiant from the cloud,
               that passes through him.

The Thrones
(Falmouth Swimming Pool)

Ghost may pour
                from any object
                              on a given day,
or sit still, emanation
                of its throne
                              until evaporated;
The headland reclines
                like a lady smoker
                              puffing out changeable
Casts of her interior;
                certain clouds emerge
                              from woodland caverns
And follow the child home
                who returns past the sulphuric
                              peace of the cliffs,
The inverse church-spire
                of the well in the
                              cottage garden;
Hard-edged inscribed clouds issue
                from the tombs like thrones
                              in the shape of small
Galleons in full sail
                setting forth on the open sky:
                              ship after ship launched
From boulder, rock and sandgrain until

       the whole town is rigged in mist;
          then the cloud-cover breaks
And the major galleons left sail
     sail high above, stealing away
         with their exchequers full of rain
The sun setting touches them, they light up
     like presences feasting in high silence;
         and the swimming pool,
Like a coal-black throne, the swimming portal
     that lights the night up
         out of which ghost
Pours into the town
    in the form of fresh, of
        newly incarnated swimmers.

From the Good People

With my naturalist's lens peering
At slipper-of-fur willowbuds, saw
Spiritface in the hooded bud,

Joyous small tree-face, I cried
'Bless you! Bless you!'
And the face aged and withered,

De-formed. I said again
Bless you! and the look changed
Back to joyousface

Tucked in the hood
Of the grey-green fur
Of the willow-bud,

Birthface in fur tippet
Furry pointed hat
Fur scarf and overcoat

In the chill spring morning
That blessed me,
Blessed me by willow-wand and dawn-ice,

Which fell like a glass mask of the
Speaking bud;
The flowerface drank this dew.

Gynandromorphism in Butterflies and Caftans

Gynandromorphism in butterflies,
                one wing coloured male,
                              the other, female;
One quite moony, the other
                brisk yellow,
                              their flight together,
Even. More male than female
                spins circles left to right;
                              the other limping flight,
Solely female-cycle.
                Giant Owl butterflies
                              of the American tropics mate
On silver-lined nettles called
                Green Silver-Lines;
                              every nettle
Has a silver lining. Now his collar opens
                and he flutters forth.
                              all the cricketers
Fluttering like butterflies
                like butterflies on a green bush:
                              the programme of the willow-game.
His silk suit a silent and mothy cocoon
                spun by how many moths
                              for how long by the clock.
The power-clothes with
                hoisted shoulders and expanded chest

        for full bellowing of his wish,
The barrel-chested suit
    that wears him, that gradually
        wears him out.
Ideally, a shirt like
    a mystical outrider
        and correct servitor,
Depending on the buttoning,
    dressed to the left or right
        you fly this way,
That, on whichever wing
    the garments decide upon,
        together or apart.
He wrenches his collar open
    for a heroic gesture, but she
        unbuttons silently
To the baby; the manchest
    blazes like a steamy grainstore
        she discloses her breasty satin-silk,
And the baby clamps tight;
    in these moments nobody
        depends on garments.
He chooses a caftan if he's flush,
    if skint, clean rags
        for the multiplex slashing
And openings, the rending of the garments
    and variety of skin rhythms, visions;
        garbed thus

He joins the funeral cortege but they
                        pelt him with the corpse's flowers,
                                          or clothed in so many rags
He runs into the mountain of flowers
               and vanishes.

The Sublime Art of Reading with Books or Without

I.

A room lined with doors from floor
                to ceiling
                              Books as backdoors
Books as scenery
                crack open the boards
                              and within that calm inside
Black prints melt off the white snow
                and a village with its green paths
                              builds of its own accord
With an author standing
                waiting on the village path
                              his grip dry and warm
And short on flesh;
                scenery in which the dead
                              and living walk
The scenery charged
                with rumours of ghosts
                              this house
Fits together on hooks
                and hinges, lift the flats apart
                              you have a library
Turned into a village street
                or parlour,
                              spaces which require
Readers who are now actors

                and actions, astonishing
                              to prop a whole life history
Putting the books back on shelves
                having found both the living
                              and the dead arrive
Because you put out
                the calculated scenery for them,
                              the right houses
The right books
                the right dead.

II.

You sleep nude between
                the featureless sheets,
                              something enters
The horn-lantern of your body
                and starts to project
                              dreams all around you
You are in the centre
                of this play, most of which
                              you forget –
Waking I hope to complete the story
                by following the numbers
                              printed on the invisible
Pages of things –
                you leap out of bed nude
                              and do a few exercises;

You then choose flexible pieces of scenery
                called clothes, hang them
                              and hinge them to your body;
Now you are a completed story
                broadcasting its signal
                              to others who attend.

Zinc Bin

The zinc bin under the
                speculative green oak
                              composed of fretted leaves
That resemble the ice crystals
                of the zinc bin.
                              Leaf stares
At leaf. I sense
                the well that is
                              present under
Its hatch, its
                stone shaft.
                              Metals like leaf in their
All-crystal, bright
                as sheared tin
                              shed an everlasting and individual
Perfume, like
                a crystal of oak leaves,
                              a hero-wreath
That is permanent.
                A street-official
                              pours a paper
Of dry sand
                into the bin with
                              the sound of rain
And a shower starts
                that drips through

                              the crystals of the oak
Creating spectra.

Floral Dentist

I.

To be afraid of the gods,
        or at least to show your fear,
                might be taken by them as an insult;
The act of sitting down at the desk
        with a pen and a vase of flowers
              is signalling to holigoste;
And four fold Adam says: turn off the drill,
        you must come and sit down
              in this rose-coloured bath with me.
The possessed dentist

        chose to reply
               in his sweet womanly voice.
He flew into the
        Rock of Jehovah,
              the silex of silence
Of Jehovah; I saw him picking at the great stones for their utterance
        in the churchyard and at the pillars
              of the transept
With one of his fine probes:
        'Fossils', he explained, 'stonescript';
              But I am sure he wanted to fill
The cavity inside the church
        with something more than song.
              Meanwhile, inside, the singer

Was dowsing out the spirit
                      that grazes like a gazelle
                                        among the flowers of technique.
Her open neck disclosed
                      the passage of Venus, in the notch
                                  above the breastbone:
It was gesticulating like a Punch-and-Judy show,
                      the two large tendons
                                  cudgelling each other
With an ultimate tenderness and throatglow;
                      I take it that the song
                                  charged up the vapours
Riding from her lungs and lights
                      and passing upwards over her bosoms.
                                  The flowers on the altar
Stared back at her, singing also
                      but without audible melody:
                                  at some stage I could hear
The colours joining in;
                      they stare back with radiant metals,
                                  their whole self
In their faces; this
                      inspires the coloratura.
                                  He fingers his skin tenderly,
He begins to think about lips
                      and rosy tongues and less
                                  about enamel, he wipes
His face with a refreshing dental cloth,

      he enters the sonorous cavity
          like a bad breath
Which is soon overcome.

II.
The flowers turn inside-out, into
      scriptures, they read these scriptures
          and the scriptures
Read them back. Routine
     so interferes with
         one's sense of reality;
One must say constantly: 'This is not
      a door, this is not
         a house, this is not
A book, I found it
      among the groves and the graves,
         where fountains of ghost
Rise from every flower, conversible ghost,
      in upgoing speech. I took the liberty
         of bringing some indoors
For the altar, and they altered everything, just
     as your "alter" is your
         other self.'

III.

Parents cause their children
        to be amazed, bring them
                to the Punch-and-Judy show
Or to the colourable songs in church,
        to feed on the milk
                of their astonishment.
But do we bring in flowers
        from the churchyard, or do they
                bring us indoors?
The church is full of sonorous filling;
        the dentist is now more than
                satisfied, and his sweet
Womanly voice is now
        his permanent possession.
                Some fragments remain
Untransformed; the self-murderer
        was excused and laid to rest here;
                he threshed the spirit
From his slovenly corpse that
        lies here making flowers and some music:
                after the struggle,
You know, they relax into death
        with the sound of popping
                all along the spine
As the rope stretches it: terminal pianism.

On the Dining-Room Shelf at Rock

An ostrich-egg
                wedged in a great
                              egg-cup, the size
Of my daughter's pelvis; a clean
                decanter like an empty diamond
                              its facets plateglass,
Its stooper brilliant-cut;
                it must have been an angel drunk from it
                              when it was an ordinary bottle,
For it is always full of light now
                decanted from the sun in the south,
                              you can taste the light
From this angel-flask.
                By contrast the opaque Chinese
                              sealed porcelain winejar next to it
Looks likely to carry within
                a genius or a yellow snake,
                              being painted so vividly with landscape:
It seems our world is its contents
                shining through its glaze like train windows
                              speeding past you if you drink up
Its memorious potion;
                And cork cubes carved into nano-shrines
                              among desiccated flower-beds,
Paused like the shuck of a thinking
                insect, discarding its latest

                              pagoda... and a fruit dish
Engraved with compasses, propped on the wall
                    so the masonic eye in the centre
                                        of the triangle glares out:
These visionary implements
                    are the hotel's at Rock, on the long
                                        shelf in the dining-room,
At the shore of the sunlit table-cloth,
                    as I in reverie wait for my full
                                        English breakfast
That muffins the five senses.

Afterglow Laboratories

I poured the dry sand
                from one broken milkbottle
                              to another –
Peterstone with all his eyes open,
                the stone made of eyes,
                              at Llandudno, in the Great Orme,
In a cliff-cavern floored
                with dry sand
                              like an alchemist
with his dry water
                ora et labora: the pouring
                              was a kind of prayer-work
I poured and repoured
                in the little warm cavern or cell,
                              poured flexible rock,
Dusty rock
                with a light in it
                              once I slipped on the turf
The Orme rolled me
                to the brink of the cliff
                              on the narrow pathway
Down from my sandlab,
                one of my laboratories.
                              I had at home another laboratory
Made of fused sand, the glassware –
                how did I gather

                                    this impressive scene
Of crystalline tubes,
            flasks, retorts,
                        fractionating columns
(An emblem of slowing the breath)
            chromotography-stripes,
                        a kind of action-painting,
The look of the glass furniture, the luminosity of
            the delicate transparent machinery
                        mattered a lot:
The transparency meant truth,
            the battles of the home revealed,
                        boiled up in these test-tubes
Like glass magic skeletons
            that healed with their fluid dance
                        their scudding drops
Made into the figures of a glitter-science
            whose haunting solvent-smells
                        of ether, of acetone tuned
Into a glass trance-device
            that bypassed
                        my father's angers
My mother's distresses.
            She combed her distresses
                        my apparatus absorbed them,
Sent them out on the air like
            dry water, and the great books
                        absorbed the anger

With their hexagonal sigils,
    for I most loved Organic Chemistry,
        its sonorous smells,
Its linked potencies.
    At Cambridge, none of the laboratories
        were mine, all were competitive
None contemplative,
    my vocation was alchemist not chemist,
        my laboratories were everywhere;
Also I could not follow
    that other ritual of fertile mud
        called Rugby Football, of chemists
Kicking a leather egg,
    much to my father's disappointment.

ALSO AVAILABLE BY PETER REDGROVE

Orchard End

The poems in *Orchard End* open up yet more magical vistas in Peter Redgrove's apparently limitless poetic house and grounds. His is a spiritual, richly imaginative and inventive art, dancing with imagery like a pond full of fish on a bright day, yet firmly based in the everyday, the here-and-now the author observes and science tries to explain. Redgrove is a shaman, a priest and healer, a seer in whose work what is all around us intimates a more hidden, abundant life. As always water and liquid find him at his best, as in 'The Mortier Water Organ', with its snaking jets and inner fountains, or the puddles and bottled rain of 'Service', a poem beautiful in its sexuality and full of puckish joie de vivre.

ISBN 1 900152 11 8 £7.50

What the Black Mirror Saw

A many-faceted composition of prose pieces that draws the reader into a Merlin's cave of revelation and delight. The partially autobiographical pieces on the creative life are especially rewarding and intriguing. One reads with the attention one willingly gives to work by Beckett, Joyce or David Jones, yet in no sense are these pieces long or difficult. The texts are descriptively evocative and vivid, conjuring up worlds reminiscent of those created by Charles Williams, or by Dylan Thomas in *Under Milk Wood*, yet clearly the author's own: worlds created in Redgrove's magic dreambag, in which images and ideas are shaken up and re-reveried. They are worlds entered with ease by way of Welsh hills, Cornish hills, Richmond Park, Malvern… or by eating oysters.

ISBN 1 900152 10 X £8.50

Abyssophone

'Streets ahead of anything else… is Peter Redgrove, one of Britain's greatest unconventional voices. Redgrove's work at first may seem surreal but there is no arbitrary image at work here. His ideas embrace Gaia, world-as-one-living organisim, the Jungian vision of the soul and the myth and magic of women as the sensual organiser of the world. *Abyssophone* sees him returning with a brilliant new Stride production while continuing his scientifically observed flight into the mesmeric realms of the unconscious.' – *New Welsh Review*

ISBN 1 900152 87 X   £6.95

The Laborators

'Peter Redgrove has been at work again in his laboratory of the human spirit, alchemising all sorts of matter into gold… In *The Laborators* the "Reader in Water at the University of Rock" as he calls himself in "Enterprise Scheme", shows once again the extraordinary fecundity of his imagination, images reproducing, dividing, proliferating with protean vitality. And he shows too that no one else has the same ability to deal with the weightiest and most elemental themes of birth, sex, nature and death with quite his lightness of touch. With his angels and spirits and depictions of all kinds of energy, Redgrove is as bold and wise as Blake, and breezier with it.'
– *Stand*

ISBN 1 900152 47 0   £6.50

These books are available, post free, from
STRIDE , 11 SYLVAN ROAD, EXETER, DEVON EX4 6EW, ENGLAND

ALSO AVAILABLE FROM STRIDE

Lady Chapel Sarah Law

The Lady Chapel houses a variety of saints and sinners. Women mystics – from the medieval Hildegard of Bingen to the longsuffering Mrs Yeats – step forward and expand our ideas of the divine. Other voices, male and female, respond by exploring conditions of intimacy or isolation. The collection ends with a sequence of yoga poems, where language is stretched along with the body, offering new perspectives on our unpredictable world.

'This is one of the most surprising and exciting collections I have read in a good while.' – George Szirtes

ISBN 1 900152 88 6   £8.50

Nekyia Rose Flint

The nekyia of Odysseus relates his 'night sea journey', a term used by Jung to describe periods of descent into darkness and the stormy, dangerous voyage through them. After leaving the country of Welsh borders that she had learned to call home, Rose Flint found living in a city again a difficult experience. It was a time of changes: a growing family moving away, the alteration age brings to a woman, the stresses that time places on a marriage. And throughout the country, landscapes altering, disappearing, eroded by commerce. *Nekyia* is a meditation on these themes, connected through the metaphor of a journey within earth-centred spirituality.

'[Rose Flint's] writing is most accomplished, elegant and fluent, working unfussily, delighting in language, full of a sense of wonder.' – *Poetry Wales*

ISBN 1 900152 89 4   £8.50

These books are available, post free, from
STRIDE, 11 SYLVAN ROAD, EXETER, DEVON EX4 6EW, ENGLAND